PRINCEWILL LAGANG

Charles Koch: Architect of Modern Conservatism and Corporate Power

First published by PRINCEWILL LAGANG 2023

Copyright © 2023 by Princewill Lagang

All rights reserved. No part of this publication may be reproduced, stored or transmitted in any form or by any means, electronic, mechanical, photocopying, recording, scanning, or otherwise without written permission from the publisher. It is illegal to copy this book, post it to a website, or distribute it by any other means without permission.

Princewill Lagang asserts the moral right to be identified as the author of this work.

First edition

This book was professionally typeset on Reedsy.
Find out more at reedsy.com

Contents

1 Introduction 1
2 The Early Years 3
3 The Libertarian Visionaries 6
4 The Koch Network Ascends 8
5 The Battle for Ideological Hegemony 10
6 Political Power and Controversies 12
7 The Legacy Unfolds 14
8 Challenges and Transformations 16
9 The Koch Legacy in a Shifting America 18
10 The Next Frontier: Challenges and Opportunities 20
11 Legacy and Reflections 22
12 Continuity and Change in a Dynamic Landscape 24
13 Towards a New Horizon 27
14 Summary 29

1

Introduction

In the annals of American history, certain figures emerge whose impact transcends the boundaries of business and politics, leaving an indelible mark on the nation's trajectory. Among these influential figures is Charles Koch, a titan of industry, a mastermind of conservative philosophy, and a key architect of modern conservatism and corporate power. Born into a family that would shape the landscape of American business, Koch's journey unfolds against the backdrop of the 20th and 21st centuries, encompassing the evolution of his family's business empire, the growth of his political influence, and the controversies that have marked his legacy.

This narrative embarks on a comprehensive exploration of Charles Koch's life, his ideological convictions, and the sprawling network of influence he cultivated. From his formative years in Wichita, Kansas, to the corridors of power in Washington, D.C., we trace the intricate interplay between Koch's business acumen and his commitment to libertarian ideals. As Koch Industries transforms into a corporate behemoth, so too does Charles Koch's influence extend into realms beyond the boardroom, shaping the very fabric of American conservatism.

Each chapter unfolds as a chapter in the larger narrative of Charles Koch's life and the network he forged. From his intellectual foundations at MIT to collaborations with libertarian visionaries, the narrative traces the trajectory of the Koch network's ascent. As the political climate shifts, we witness the network's strategic involvement in elections, policy battles, and the broader conservative movement. The evolving landscape of American society, marked by technological advancements, changing demographics, and pressing environmental concerns, becomes the backdrop against which the Koch legacy unfolds.

Yet, this narrative is not just a chronicle of success and influence; it also delves into the controversies that have surrounded Charles Koch and the network. From allegations of undue influence to debates about the role of money in politics, we navigate the challenges that have shaped and, at times, threatened the Koch legacy.

As the narrative progresses through each chapter, it aims to provide a comprehensive understanding of the forces that have shaped Charles Koch's life, the evolution of the Koch network, and the enduring impact on American conservatism, libertarian thought, and the intersection of business and ideology. The story serves as a lens through which to explore the intricate relationships between wealth, power, and political influence in the United States.

2

The Early Years

Title: Charles Koch: Architect of Modern Conservatism and Corporate Power

In the quiet town of Wichita, Kansas, on November 1, 1935, Charles de Ganahl Koch was born into a family that would play a significant role in shaping the political and economic landscape of the United States. As the second son of Fred C. Koch, an industrialist and founder of Koch Industries, Charles inherited a legacy that would propel him into the forefront of modern conservatism and corporate power.

The Koch family was no stranger to the complexities of business and the influence it wielded in society. Fred Koch, a chemical engineer, founded Koch Industries in 1940, initially focusing on oil refining and chemical production. The company's early success set the stage for Charles Koch's introduction to the world of business and politics.

Growing up in an environment that emphasized the values of free-market capitalism and limited government intervention, Charles Koch developed a keen interest in the intersection of business and politics from an early age. His father's strong anti-communist sentiments and belief in individual freedom left a lasting impact on young Charles, shaping his worldview and laying the groundwork for his future endeavors.

As a student at the Massachusetts Institute of Technology (MIT), Charles Koch delved into the fields of engineering and economics. It was during this time that he began to refine his understanding of the principles that would later become the cornerstones of his political philosophy. The intellectual ferment of MIT's academic environment, coupled with his father's business acumen, fueled Koch's ambition to merge his passion for free-market ideals with practical business strategies.

Upon completing his education, Charles Koch joined the family business, where he embarked on a mission to expand and diversify Koch Industries. Under his leadership, the company evolved into a sprawling conglomerate with interests in energy, chemicals, finance, and more. As Koch Industries flourished, so did Charles Koch's influence on the national stage.

Simultaneously, Charles Koch became increasingly involved in libertarian and conservative circles. He embraced the ideas of thinkers like Friedrich Hayek and Milton Friedman, advocating for minimal government interference, individual liberty, and free-market capitalism. Koch saw his business success as intertwined with his ideological mission – to reshape the political landscape in alignment with his vision.

The confluence of Koch's business acumen and political ideology came to the fore as he became a major financier of conservative causes and think tanks. Organizations like the Cato Institute and the Heritage Foundation found a benefactor in Charles Koch, whose financial support helped amplify their messages and advance the principles of limited government and free-market capitalism.

Chapter 1 sets the stage for the intricate interplay between Charles Koch's upbringing, education, and the ideological currents that would propel him into a role as a leading architect of modern conservatism and corporate power. The narrative explores the early influences that shaped his worldview and the convergence of business and politics that defined his trajectory.

3

The Libertarian Visionaries

Title: Forging Alliances and Shaping Ideology

As Charles Koch solidified his position at the helm of Koch Industries, he recognized the need for a broader network to advance his libertarian ideals. Chapter 2 delves into the alliances and intellectual collaborations that Koch cultivated to bolster his influence on both the political and ideological fronts.

In the late 1960s and early 1970s, a pivotal era in American politics, Charles Koch sought kindred spirits who shared his vision of limited government and free-market principles. His interactions with like-minded intellectuals, including economists, philosophers, and political theorists, marked the genesis of a movement that would come to be known as libertarianism.

The Mont Pelerin Society, a global organization of economists and intellectuals founded by Friedrich Hayek, became a crucial forum for Koch's ideological pursuits. Through his involvement in the society, Koch engaged with prominent thinkers, exchanging ideas and refining the intellectual foundations of his political philosophy. The society's annual meetings became a breeding ground for the fusion of libertarian theory and practical political strategies.

This chapter explores Charles Koch's interactions with influential figures such as Milton Friedman, Friedrich Hayek, and Robert Nozick. It delves into the intellectual ferment of these collaborations, examining how these libertarian visionaries shaped Koch's understanding of the role of government, individual rights, and the free market.

As Koch Industries continued to grow, so did Charles Koch's commitment to translating his ideological beliefs into tangible political outcomes. He strategically directed resources toward think tanks, academic institutions, and advocacy groups that aligned with his libertarian vision. The Institute for Humane Studies and the Mercatus Center emerged as key recipients of Koch's financial support, playing pivotal roles in shaping libertarian thought and influencing policy.

Simultaneously, Chapter 2 explores Koch's engagement with political activism. His financial backing of political candidates who embraced libertarian principles marked a strategic shift toward influencing policy at a more direct level. The chapter traces the evolution of Koch's involvement in electoral politics, from local campaigns to broader national initiatives.

By the end of the 1970s, Charles Koch had positioned himself as a driving force behind the libertarian movement, using his wealth and influence to reshape the American political landscape. Chapter 2 illuminates the pivotal role played by intellectual collaborations and strategic alliances in Charles Koch's journey from a businessman with libertarian convictions to a key architect of modern conservatism and corporate power.

4

The Koch Network Ascends

Title: Building a Political and Corporate Empire

As the 1980s dawned, Charles Koch's influence extended beyond the realm of ideas and intellectual collaborations. Chapter 3 delves into the expansion of the Koch network, both in terms of political activism and corporate power, as Charles Koch navigated the changing landscape of American politics and business.

The chapter begins with the political climate of the 1980s, marked by the election of Ronald Reagan and the ascendancy of conservative ideologies. Charles Koch seized the opportunity to amplify his influence by strategically aligning with the burgeoning conservative movement. His financial support for conservative candidates, advocacy groups, and think tanks increased, solidifying his role as a major player in shaping the direction of the Republican Party.

Simultaneously, Koch Industries continued its ascent under Charles's leadership. The company's diversified portfolio expanded into new sectors, cementing its status as one of the largest privately-owned corporations in the United States. The chapter explores the symbiotic relationship between Koch's political activism and his business interests, revealing how the success of one bolstered the other.

One of the key features of the Koch network was its decentralized and multifaceted approach to political influence. The chapter examines the establishment of entities like Americans for Prosperity (AFP) and the Cato Institute, organizations that became instrumental in advancing Koch's libertarian and conservative agenda. These entities allowed Koch to influence public policy, promote free-market principles, and shape the narrative around limited government.

Chapter 3 also delves into the controversies surrounding the Koch network. As the influence of Koch-backed groups grew, so did scrutiny and criticism. Detractors accused the Kochs of using their immense wealth to unduly influence elections and policy decisions, sparking debates about the role of money in politics and the boundaries between corporate interests and public governance.

The chapter concludes with an analysis of the lasting impact of Charles Koch's dual pursuits: building a political empire rooted in libertarian ideals and expanding a corporate behemoth that exerted influence across various sectors. The Koch network's rise during this period laid the groundwork for future chapters, where the intersection of politics, ideology, and corporate power would continue to shape the course of American history.

5

The Battle for Ideological Hegemony

Title: Koch's Influence on Public Opinion and Policy

Entering the 21st century, Charles Koch's influence extended beyond the confines of traditional political channels. Chapter 4 explores the Koch network's strategic efforts to shape public opinion and influence policy through a multifaceted approach that included media, think tanks, and educational initiatives.

The chapter opens with an examination of the Kochs' foray into media and public relations. Recognizing the power of narrative in shaping public opinion, Charles Koch increased his investments in media outlets sympathetic to his libertarian and conservative ideologies. The creation of The Washington Times and financial support for outlets like Reason magazine became instrumental in advancing the Koch network's messaging and countering what they perceived as liberal biases in mainstream media.

In parallel, the Kochs expanded their influence within academic circles. The establishment of programs and institutes at universities across the country aimed to promote the study and dissemination of free-market economic principles. The chapter delves into the controversies surrounding these academic initiatives, exploring debates over academic independence, intellectual diversity, and the role of private funding in shaping university curricula.

Americans for Prosperity (AFP), a key player in the Koch network, took center stage in grassroots activism. The chapter explores how AFP mobilized supporters, organized rallies, and lobbied for policies aligned with Koch's vision of limited government. The network's involvement in state-level politics, particularly in battleground states, showcased its commitment to reshaping policy from the ground up.

Another significant aspect of Chapter 4 is the Koch network's engagement with philanthropy. The Charles Koch Foundation and the Charles Koch Institute emerged as major contributors to educational and research initiatives, further solidifying the Kochs' influence in shaping the ideological landscape. The chapter analyzes how this philanthropic approach intertwined with the broader goals of the Koch network, influencing both public opinion and policy discussions.

However, the rise of the Koch network was met with increasing opposition. Critics questioned the ethical implications of billionaires wielding such significant influence over public discourse and policy decisions. The chapter explores the challenges and controversies that emerged as the Kochs faced heightened scrutiny, with some viewing their activities as a threat to democratic principles.

Chapter 4 concludes by examining the ongoing battle for ideological hegemony, where the Koch network's efforts to shape public opinion and policy faced both successes and setbacks. As the narrative unfolds, it becomes clear that Charles Koch's vision extended beyond mere economic interests, encompassing a comprehensive strategy to reshape American society in line with his libertarian principles.

6

Political Power and Controversies

Title: The Koch Network in the Age of Polarization

As the United States entered an era marked by increasing political polarization, Chapter 5 explores the evolution of the Koch network's influence, its deepening involvement in electoral politics, and the controversies that accompanied its quest for ideological dominance.

The chapter begins by examining the heightened political polarization that characterized the early 21st century. Against this backdrop, the Koch network intensified its efforts to shape the political landscape by strategically supporting candidates who aligned with its libertarian and conservative principles. The chapter delves into the network's role in funding political campaigns, contributing to the rise of candidates at various levels of government who championed limited government, deregulation, and free-market policies.

At the heart of this political involvement was the network's approach to elections. The chapter explores the establishment and activities of political advocacy groups like Americans for Prosperity (AFP) and Freedom Partners, entities that played pivotal roles in electoral politics. These organizations mobilized grassroots support, launched targeted advertising campaigns, and influenced voter turnout, contributing to the electoral successes of candidates sympathetic to the Koch network's agenda.

Simultaneously, the chapter investigates the controversies surrounding the Koch network's political activities. Accusations of dark money, the undisclosed funding of political campaigns, and the perceived erosion of transparency in the electoral process fueled public and political debates. The Kochs' network became a focal point in discussions about campaign finance reform, with critics arguing that such vast financial influence undermined the democratic principles of equal representation.

The chapter also delves into the network's engagement with high-profile policy battles, including its opposition to the Affordable Care Act (ACA) and efforts to roll back environmental regulations. Charles Koch's strategic funding of think tanks, advocacy groups, and legal initiatives played a crucial role in shaping public opinion and influencing policy decisions, particularly during pivotal moments in the legislative process.

Furthermore, Chapter 5 explores the network's response to the changing dynamics within the Republican Party. The rise of the Tea Party movement and the subsequent intra-party conflicts highlighted the complex interplay between ideological purists and establishment figures, with the Koch network often positioned at the nexus of these tensions.

As the chapter unfolds, it becomes clear that the Koch network's pursuit of political power was not without challenges and controversies. The narrative captures the ongoing struggles and successes of Charles Koch and his network in an era defined by deepening ideological divisions and an evolving political landscape.

7

The Legacy Unfolds

Title: Koch Industries, Philanthropy, and the Shaping of American Discourse

Entering the second decade of the 21st century, Chapter 6 delves into the multifaceted legacy of Charles Koch, examining the continued expansion of Koch Industries, the family's philanthropic endeavors, and the lasting impact of the Koch network on American political and economic discourse.

The chapter begins with an exploration of Koch Industries' continued growth and diversification. Under Charles Koch's leadership, the company expanded its reach into new industries, solidifying its position as one of the largest privately-owned corporations in the world. The narrative examines the challenges and successes that accompanied this growth, shedding light on the evolving dynamics of the business empire Charles Koch inherited from his father.

Simultaneously, the chapter explores the philanthropic initiatives championed by Charles Koch and the broader Koch family. The establishment of the Koch Cultural Trust, the Charles Koch Foundation, and other charitable entities underscored the family's commitment to supporting educational and cultural endeavors. This section of the narrative delves into the impact of Koch's philanthropy on academic research, public policy, and societal discourse.

The Koch network's influence on education receives particular attention, examining the establishment of research centers, academic programs, and think tanks that furthered libertarian and free-market ideas. The chapter also explores controversies surrounding the influence of the Kochs within academic institutions, touching on debates about intellectual freedom, academic independence, and the role of private funding in shaping educational agendas.

The chapter then transitions to an analysis of Charles Koch's advocacy for criminal justice reform. His unexpected alignment with liberal figures on issues such as mass incarceration and sentencing reform showcased a pragmatic approach that diverged from traditional conservative positions. The narrative delves into the motivations behind Koch's stance on criminal justice and its implications for broader political alliances.

The latter part of Chapter 6 examines the political landscape in the wake of Charles Koch's advancing age. The narrative considers the future of the Koch network, acknowledging the generational transition within the family and its potential impact on the trajectory of their political and business activities.

Ultimately, as the chapter concludes, it reflects on the lasting imprint of Charles Koch on American conservatism, libertarian thought, and corporate influence. The narrative examines the complexities of his legacy, the ongoing debates surrounding the Koch network, and the ways in which Charles Koch's vision continues to shape the contours of American discourse in the realms of politics, economics, and philanthropy.

8

Challenges and Transformations

Title: Navigating the Shifting Sands of American Politics

As the second decade of the 21st century unfolded, the Koch network faced a series of challenges and transformations. Chapter 7 explores how external dynamics, internal shifts, and the broader political climate influenced the trajectory of the Kochs' influence in American politics and society.

The chapter opens with an examination of the changing political landscape, marked by the rise of populism and shifts within the Republican Party. The Koch network, which had played a significant role in shaping conservative ideologies, found itself navigating new challenges posed by the unconventional politics of the time. The narrative explores the network's responses to the rise of figures like Donald Trump and the ideological shifts within the GOP.

Simultaneously, the chapter delves into the internal dynamics of the Koch family and network. With the passing of David Koch in 2019, the narrative examines the implications of this loss on the family's political activities and philanthropic initiatives. It considers how generational transitions and changes in leadership within the network impacted its strategies and priorities.

The political and ideological battles of the era are a focal point of Chapter 7. The narrative explores the Koch network's involvement in pivotal policy debates, including healthcare reform, tax policy, and environmental regulations. It analyzes the successes and setbacks the network experienced in influencing policy decisions at both the state and national levels.

The chapter also addresses the Koch network's evolving stance on environmental issues. Charles Koch's public statements acknowledging the reality of climate change and advocating for market-driven solutions demonstrate a departure from traditional conservative positions. The narrative examines how this shift impacted the network's relationships with both political allies and adversaries.

In addition, Chapter 7 explores the network's efforts to expand its influence in new arenas, such as technology and data analytics. The narrative investigates how the Kochs embraced innovative strategies to shape public opinion, influence elections, and advance their political agenda in an increasingly digital and interconnected world.

As the chapter progresses, it analyzes the challenges posed by increased scrutiny and criticism of the Koch network. The narrative explores how the family's influence faced backlash from various quarters, raising questions about the role of money in politics, corporate influence, and the integrity of democratic processes.

The concluding sections of Chapter 7 reflect on the state of the Koch network as it adapts to the evolving political and societal landscape. The narrative considers the enduring impact of the network's decades-long influence and speculates on its future role in shaping American politics and discourse.

9

The Koch Legacy in a Shifting America

Title: Reckoning with Influence and Shaping the Future

As the 2020s unfolded, Chapter 8 explores the legacy of the Koch network in the context of an America grappling with socio-political shifts, technological advancements, and an evolving understanding of corporate influence. This chapter provides a comprehensive assessment of the lasting impact of Charles Koch's vision on the nation and examines the network's response to contemporary challenges.

The narrative begins by examining the Koch network's role in the 2020 presidential election. The chapter explores the strategies employed, the candidates supported, and the ideological battles within a Republican Party undergoing transformation. It delves into how the network navigated the complexities of a deeply polarized political environment, where traditional alliances were being reshaped.

In the wake of the 2020 election, the chapter addresses the Koch network's engagement with the Biden administration. It explores areas of potential collaboration and opposition, shedding light on how the network adapted its strategies in response to shifts in political power.

The narrative also delves into the Koch network's continued efforts to influence policy at the state level. As states increasingly became battlegrounds for key policy decisions, the network's focus on local and regional politics gained prominence. The chapter analyzes the successes and challenges faced by the Kochs in advancing their agenda at the state level.

One of the key aspects of Chapter 8 is an examination of the evolving nature of corporate activism and social responsibility. The narrative explores how the Koch network responded to changing expectations regarding corporate engagement in societal issues. It considers the network's efforts to shape the discourse around corporate influence, responsibility, and the role of businesses in addressing social and environmental challenges.

The chapter also addresses the Koch network's response to pressing global issues, including the ongoing challenges posed by climate change. It explores how the network's evolving stance on environmental issues reflects broader shifts within the conservative movement and corporate America.

In addition, Chapter 8 reflects on the controversies and criticisms that have accompanied the Koch legacy. It examines how public perception and scrutiny of the network have influenced its strategies and activities, shedding light on the ongoing debate about the role of money in politics.

The concluding sections of the chapter contemplate the future of the Koch legacy in a rapidly changing America. The narrative considers the potential trajectories of the Koch network, its influence on conservative and libertarian thought, and the enduring questions about the role of wealthy individuals and corporations in shaping the nation's destiny.

10

The Next Frontier: Challenges and Opportunities

Title: Navigating a Complex Landscape

As the narrative progresses into the latter part of the 2020s, Chapter 9 explores the challenges and opportunities facing the Koch network in a landscape defined by rapid technological advancements, shifting demographics, and ongoing socio-political transformations. This chapter provides insights into how the Kochs are adapting to the complexities of a new era while continuing to shape the contours of American discourse.

The chapter begins by examining the network's response to the digital age. It explores how the Kochs are leveraging technology, data analytics, and social media to amplify their influence, mobilize support, and shape public opinion. The narrative delves into the network's evolving strategies in an era where information dissemination and political engagement occur at an unprecedented pace.

Demographic changes and shifting societal norms also take center stage

THE NEXT FRONTIER: CHALLENGES AND OPPORTUNITIES

in Chapter 9. The narrative explores how the Koch network is adapting its messaging and policy priorities to resonate with a changing America. It delves into the network's efforts to address issues of social justice, diversity, and inclusivity while staying true to its core principles of free-market capitalism and limited government.

The chapter further explores the Kochs' engagement with philanthropy and social impact initiatives. It examines how the family is leveraging its wealth to address pressing societal challenges, including education, healthcare, and economic inequality. The narrative considers the impact of these initiatives on the Koch legacy and the broader discourse around the responsibilities of the wealthy in shaping societal well-being.

The political landscape remains a focal point, with the narrative examining the Koch network's role in shaping electoral outcomes, influencing policy decisions, and navigating the continued evolution of the Republican Party. As new leaders emerge and political dynamics shift, the chapter analyzes how the network positions itself to remain a potent force in American politics.

A crucial aspect of Chapter 9 is the network's approach to environmental sustainability. The narrative explores how the Kochs are responding to increasing calls for corporate responsibility in addressing climate change. It delves into the network's stance on environmental policies, clean energy, and the role of businesses in mitigating the impacts of climate change.

The concluding sections of the chapter reflect on the enduring legacy of Charles Koch and the Koch network. It considers the impact of their influence on American conservatism, libertarian thought, and corporate activism. The narrative speculates on the future trajectory of the Koch network and its role in shaping the discourse of a nation navigating the challenges and opportunities of a new era.

11

Legacy and Reflections

Title: Enduring Influences on American Ideals

As the story approaches its conclusion, Chapter 10 reflects on the lasting legacy of Charles Koch and the Koch network, examining their enduring influences on American ideals, politics, and the intersection of business and ideology. This final chapter provides a comprehensive overview of the network's impact, its evolution over time, and the broader implications of its legacy for the nation.

The narrative begins by revisiting key milestones in the life of Charles Koch, tracing his journey from a young businessman with libertarian convictions to a major architect of modern conservatism and corporate power. It reflects on the challenges and triumphs that marked this trajectory, acknowledging the complexities inherent in Charles Koch's vision and influence.

The chapter explores the transformation of the Koch network over the years, considering its responses to shifting political landscapes, societal changes, and the evolving nature of corporate influence. It delves into the ways in which the network adapted its strategies, navigated controversies, and maintained its position as a powerful force in American politics and discourse.

A significant portion of Chapter 10 is dedicated to examining the broader impact of the Koch legacy on the conservative movement and the Republican Party. The narrative considers how the network's influence shaped policy debates, electoral outcomes, and the ideological direction of the conservative agenda. It reflects on the role of the Kochs in fostering a fusion of economic libertarianism, social conservatism, and corporate interests within the broader conservative coalition.

The chapter also addresses the criticisms and controversies that have accompanied the Koch network throughout its existence. It reflects on the debates surrounding campaign finance, corporate influence in politics, and the implications of concentrated wealth on democratic processes. The narrative acknowledges the challenges faced by the Kochs in reconciling their vision with the diverse and dynamic landscape of American society.

In addition to political and economic influences, Chapter 10 explores the cultural and intellectual impact of the Koch network. It considers the network's contributions to libertarian thought, academic research, and public policy discussions. The narrative reflects on the ways in which the Kochs shaped the discourse around limited government, free-market capitalism, and individual liberty.

The concluding sections of the chapter reflect on the future of the Koch legacy. The narrative considers the ongoing role of the Koch network in American politics, philanthropy, and business. It speculates on the enduring impact of Charles Koch's vision on shaping the nation's trajectory in the years to come.

Chapter 10 serves as a thoughtful reflection on the complex legacy of Charles Koch and the Koch network, offering readers a nuanced understanding of their enduring influences on the American political landscape and societal discourse.

12

Continuity and Change in a Dynamic Landscape

Title: Navigating the Unpredictable Future

As the narrative extends into the unfolding years, Chapter 11 explores how the Koch network continues to navigate an ever-evolving American landscape. Faced with unprecedented challenges and opportunities, this chapter delves into the strategies, decisions, and adaptations that define the network's role in shaping the nation's future.

The chapter begins by examining the network's response to emerging global challenges. Whether it be the ongoing ramifications of the COVID-19 pandemic, geopolitical shifts, or economic uncertainties, the narrative explores how the Koch network positions itself as a dynamic force capable of addressing the complex issues facing the United States and the world.

In the realm of technology and communication, Chapter 11 delves into the network's engagement with the digital age. The narrative explores how advancements in technology, social media, and data analytics influence the network's strategies in shaping public opinion, mobilizing supporters, and advocating for its libertarian and conservative principles.

Demographic changes and shifting societal norms continue to play a pivotal role in American politics. The chapter reflects on how the Koch network adapts its messaging, policy priorities, and engagement strategies to resonate with an evolving and diversifying population. The narrative considers the network's stance on social justice issues and its efforts to bridge ideological divides in a polarized society.

As political landscapes transform, the chapter explores the Koch network's continued involvement in electoral politics. It considers the network's strategies in supporting candidates, influencing policy decisions, and navigating the evolving dynamics within the Republican Party. The narrative reflects on how the network positions itself in a political environment marked by shifting alliances and ideological realignments.

Philanthropy remains a central aspect of the Koch legacy, and Chapter 11 examines how the family continues to leverage its wealth for social impact. The narrative explores the network's philanthropic initiatives in education, healthcare, and societal well-being, considering how these efforts align with evolving societal needs and expectations.

Environmental sustainability remains a critical focus, and the chapter delves into the Koch network's position on climate change and clean energy. It explores how the network navigates the intersection of economic interests, environmental responsibility, and public expectations in an era increasingly shaped by environmental concerns.

The concluding sections of Chapter 11 offer reflections on the continued relevance and influence of the Koch network. The narrative considers the challenges and opportunities that lie ahead, speculating on the role the network might play in shaping the future direction of American politics, business, and ideological discourse.

Chapter 11 serves as a bridge between the Koch network's storied past and the unfolding chapters of its future, offering insights into how this influential force navigates the complexities of an ever-changing and unpredictable landscape.

13

Towards a New Horizon

Title: Legacy, Challenges, and the Ongoing Impact

As the narrative approaches its conclusion, Chapter 12 provides a retrospective view of the Koch network's enduring impact on American politics, economics, and societal discourse. This chapter reflects on the legacy of Charles Koch, the network's evolution over time, and the challenges and opportunities that shape its ongoing influence.

The narrative revisits key moments in the Koch network's history, tracing its origins, pivotal milestones, and transformations. It reflects on the contributions of Charles Koch to conservative thought, libertarian philosophy, and the intersection of business and politics. The chapter considers how the network's activities have shaped the broader landscape of American political and economic ideologies.

One central theme of Chapter 12 is the ongoing relevance of the Koch network. The narrative explores how the principles and strategies established by Charles Koch continue to influence political debates, policy decisions, and the direction of the conservative movement. It considers the network's adaptive capacities in response to evolving societal norms, political dynamics, and economic challenges.

The chapter delves into the philanthropic efforts of the Koch family and network, examining how their contributions have impacted education, research, and various social initiatives. It reflects on the motivations behind their philanthropy and the legacy they aim to leave in areas beyond politics and business.

Environmental considerations and the Koch network's response to global challenges are key focal points in Chapter 12. The narrative explores how the network addresses environmental sustainability, acknowledging the shifting expectations regarding corporate responsibility in the face of climate change and other ecological concerns.

Challenges and criticisms faced by the Koch network are not overlooked. The chapter considers controversies surrounding campaign finance, allegations of undue influence, and the ongoing debates about the role of wealth in American democracy. It reflects on how the network has navigated these challenges and adapted its strategies over time.

A significant aspect of Chapter 12 is the examination of the generational transition within the Koch family and network. As new leaders emerge, the narrative explores how the network continues to navigate internal dynamics, sustain its core principles, and foster a vision for the future.

In conclusion, Chapter 12 provides a comprehensive reflection on the Koch network's legacy and the ongoing impact of Charles Koch's vision. It considers the enduring influence of the network on American conservatism, libertarian thought, and the intersection of business and ideology. The chapter also speculates on the future trajectory of the Koch network and its role in shaping the evolving landscape of American politics and society.

14

Summary

In this comprehensive narrative spanning twelve chapters, we explore the life and legacy of Charles Koch, examining his role as an architect of modern conservatism and corporate power. The story begins with Koch's early years in Wichita, Kansas, shaped by his father's industrial success and anti-communist ideals. Chapter by chapter, we follow Koch's intellectual development at MIT, his engagement with libertarian visionaries, and the formation of the Koch network. As Koch Industries grows, so does his influence, expanding into politics, media, and academia.

The narrative navigates the network's involvement in elections, policy battles, and controversies, exploring its impact on conservative thought and the Republican Party. We delve into the intricate interplay between Koch's business empire, political activism, and philanthropy. The story unfolds against the backdrop of a changing America, grappling with political polarization, technological advancements, and environmental concerns.

In the later chapters, we witness the network's response to emerging challenges, its forays into philanthropy, and its evolving stance on social and environmental issues. As the narrative concludes, we reflect on the enduring legacy of Charles Koch, the challenges faced by the Koch network, and its ongoing impact on American discourse and politics.

This comprehensive narrative aims to provide a nuanced understanding of Charles Koch's life, his network's multifaceted influence, and the complex interplay between ideology, business, and politics in shaping the trajectory of the United States.

www.ingramcontent.com/pod-product-compliance
Lightning Source LLC
LaVergne TN
LVHW010443070526
838199LV00066B/6163